God's Passion

A Look at the Cross

Jeffrey D. Johnson

I0808398

Wipf & Stock
PUBLISHERS
Eugene, Oregon

Wipf and Stock Publishers
199 W 8th Ave, Suite 3
Eugene, OR 97401

God's Passion
A Look at the Cross
By Johnson, Jeffrey D.

ISBN 13: 978-1-55635-080-1
ISBN 10: 1-55635-080-5
Publication date 11/30/2006

About Israel Today Ministries

Three-fold Purpose:

- Teach the Church about Israel
- Teach Israel about their Messiah
- Help feed those in need (Romans 15:27; Genesis 12:1-3)

To receive Dr. Johnson's "teaching letters," or, if you would like to send a gift to Israel Today Ministries, or if you would like Dr. Johnson to speak at your church event, school, or small group, contact:

Israel Today Ministries
P.O. Box 150288
Arlington, TX 76015
Phone/Fax 817.468.4441
E mail: Galileeman@juno.com

This is Yossef (Joseph) and Abigail. Your monthly donations help feed little ones like these.

"Inasmuch as ye have done it unto one of the least of these my brethren, ye have done it unto me" –Jesus, Matthew 25:40

About Dr. Jeffrey D. Johnson

- Three decades in ministry
- Founder/Director of Israel Today Ministries
- Director of tours to the Middle East
- Senior pastor in Ohio, Massachusetts and California
- Almost 7 years directorship with International Ministries to Israel (formerly, The American Association for Jewish Evangelism, where the famed Hyman Appelman was the first president)
- Conference speaker
- Bible expositor
- Guest lecturer
- Author

Born and raised in the Midwest, Dr. Johnson took his B.D. from Massillon Baptist College, his MA from Moody Bible Institute, and his Th.M. and Th.D. from Christian Bible College. His passion for Israel, the Jewish roots of Christianity and Bible prophecy, is well known. His teaching will stir your heart to follow the Lord and to love and *"pray for the peace of Jerusalem"* (Psalm 122:6).

As an "Itinerant Bible Teacher," Dr. Johnson will travel anywhere to proclaim God's redeeming Grace through our Lord and Savior Jesus the Messiah, *"to the Jew first, and also to the Greek"* (Romans 1:16).

His call is to *"Teach the Church about Israel; Teach Israel about their Messiah; and to feed those in need"* (Genesis 12:3; Romans 15:27).

Dr. Jeff and his wife, Louise, have purposed to serve the Lord trusting God to provide the funds and resources for their livelihood.

Israel Today Ministries, founded by Dr. Johnson, is a faith ministry, supported by "love offerings" from those desiring to bless Israel. Dr. Jeff and Louise have been commissioned and sent out by their home church.

Comments from Christian Leaders

I am pleased to recommend him to churches as an able expositor of the Word of God.

– *the late* **John Walvoord**, Chancellor,
Dallas Theological Seminary

A Bible Expositor with special insights on the origin, nature and destiny of God's chosen people, Israel.

– **John C. Whitcomb**, Bible Scholar, Author, Professor

A careful expositor of Scripture.

– **Homer Kent**, President Emeritus,
Grace College and Seminary

A practitioner of all that he preaches.

– **Paige Patterson**, former President of the
Southern Baptist Convention, President,
Southeastern Baptist Theological Seminary

He has a wonderful grasp of Jewish history and liturgy.

– **Edgar C. James**, Professor, Moody Bible Institute

He is a person who has been uniquely prepared by God to preach and teach about God's special people. Any one who hears him will come away with a great love for the people of Abraham.

–**Dick Dahlquist**, Chair, Pastoral Studies, Acting Dean,
Grace College of Graduate Studies

He has a gifted teaching ministry which encompasses Biblical prophecy and insights into modern-day Judaism.

–the late **Paul Tassell**, Bible Scholar, Author,
former National Representative of the G.A.R.B.C.

He has a great ministry.

– **LaVerne Butler**, former President of Mid-Continent Baptist College, Scholar, Conference Speaker, President, Pulpit Aflame

Your heart will be thrilled as he ministers the prophetic Scriptures.

– the late **Alden A. Gannett**, President Emeritus of Southeastern Bible College, Bible Scholar, Author, Conference Speaker, President, Gannett Ministries

He loves the people and nation of Israel. He has given himself to a thorough study of God's ancient people and of the prophetic.

– **Ivan H. French**, Pastor Emeritus, Pleasant View Bible Church, former Professor, Grace College and Seminary

The Cry

"Eli, Eli, lama sabachthani?" cried Jesus on the cross. "My God, my God, why hast thou forsaken me?" (Matthew 27:46).

At that moment Heaven stood still in awe. A paradigm shift took place. Something changed. The angels had to marvel. The heavenly beings must have gasped. For the first time in eternity, God the Father turned His face from God the Son. Why would the Father turn his face? Why? What happened? Before I endeavor to answer that question, let's go back to the beginning.

John 1:1

"In the beginning was the Word, and the Word was with God, and the Word was God."

The opening verse in the Gospel of John reminds us of the opening verse in Genesis: "In the Beginning God created the heaven and the earth." Genesis chapter one connects the Creator with the creation. Timeless eternity, non-time, before time, the eternal past, or preface to time is being referred to here. Before anything existed, God was there. Then He created.

John, in his opening statements, also connects the creator with the creation. He uses the Greek word, *"Logos"*, translated "Word." The way John uses "Logos" is to emphasize that the "Word" was the designer, genius or the mind behind the creation of the universe.

Eternally God

John then says this Logos *"was God."* The Greek word translated "was" is in the imperfect tense which means it is something continuous. It doesn't refer to something that is past, present or future, but rather, something that has no beginning or ending. It always has existed with no beginning and no ending, referencing that the Logos was the same, not "as" God, nor "a" God, but God Himself, with no beginning and no ending.

The Logos, writes John, "was made flesh and dwelt among us" (John 1:14). When John remarks about the "Word" he is speaking of Jesus. Jesus, John says, is God. Therefore, when we think of Jesus, we must think of Jesus as never having a beginning, nor never having an ending. He is eternally, equally, unquestionably God.

Face to Face

Notice in the middle of verse one of John 1:1: *"the Word was with God"*. This little word translated "with" in the Greek is *"pros"*. "Pros" means "Face to face," a sense of intimacy, interfacing, living intercourse, communion, fellowship, a similar nature or likeness and a sense of home. All of this implies separate personality and yet complete union. This boggles the mind! Verse one of John is speaking of the union of the God-head: Father, Son, & Holy Spirit, or, the Trinity.

Therefore, from the very beginning of eternity past you had the Father and the Son having eternal co-existence and unity and yet at the Cross of Calvary Jesus cried out, "My God, My God why hast thou forsaken me?" What happened?

Forsaken

The Scripture states that God cannot look upon iniquity (sin). "Thou art of purer eyes than to behold evil, and canst not look on iniquity" (Habakkuk 1:13). In fact it is recorded many times that God will hide his face from sin, thus turning His face of fellowship and blessing. (Deut. 31:18; Ps. 44:24; Isa. 1:15; 59:2; 64:7; Eze. 39:23; Micah 3:4).

When Jesus hung on the cross, He became sin. Paul said in Galatians 3:13, "Christ hath redeemed us from the curse of the law, being made a curse for us: for it is written, Cursed is every one that hangeth on a tree."

The Prophet Isaiah stated, "All we like sheep have gone astray; we have turned every one to his own way; and the Lord hath laid on him (Messiah) the iniquity of us all" (53:6).

What does this mean? It means that when Jesus was hanging there on the cross, at that very moment when he cried, "My God, My God, why hast thou forsaken me?"

it was at that moment He bore our sin, thus becoming sin (Isa. 53:12; Heb. 9:28; 1 Pet. 2:24; 1 Jn. 3:5). He became murder, adultery, lying, lust, and everything you can think of regarding the nature of sin. Therefore, the union of fellowship that the Son had with the Father from the very beginning was severed. For the first time in all eternity, God the Father turned His face from God the Son. Jesus became sin (iniquity), therefore, the Father hid His face from Jesus who became sin for us. Jesus was paying the penalty for sin, so that those who believe and trust in Him alone for salvation will receive forgiveness and eternal life with God (John 3:16).

It is finished

Moments later, Jesus said, "It is finished: and he bowed his head, and gave up the ghost" (John 19:30). Jesus died.

Do you remember when Jesus said, "I lay down my life, that I might take it again. No man taketh it from me, but I lay it down of myself. I have power to lay it down, and I have power to take it again" (John 10:17,18)? Jesus declared that nobody would kill him, but that He would choose where, how and when to die.

Wait a minute! The soldiers nailed Jesus to the cross. Yes…However, Jesus chose the moment when He would die.

During this time of year the Jews were getting ready for the Passover. It is said that approximately one million Jews from all over the known world would have come to Jerusalem to celebrate this holiday that remembers the Jewish Exodus out of Egypt and all the miracles God manifested in Egypt and the wilderness. You remember the Ten Commandments with Charleston Heston playing the role of Moses?

Part of the tradition and celebration included the head of each household taking a lamb to the Temple to be slaughtered as a sacrifice unto the Lord. Each family would procure a lamb and tend to it making sure it was without spot or blemish.

Then at the appointed time on the day of Passover, the heads of the households, wearing a special white outer garment, would carry the lamb on their shoulders into the Temple. They would line up by the thousands.

At 3:00 P.M., the time of the afternoon sacrifice, a priest would climb to the top of the wall and blow the shofar (trumpet) indicating that it was time to offer the Passover Lamb. The heads of the households would take a special sacrificial knife and slit the lamb's throat. The priests, who were standing by, would catch the blood in a basin and then offer the blood upon the Altar. The men would prepare the lamb and take it home to be eaten with family and friends.

The blood would splatter on the white garments worn by the men. They would walk home with this blood stained outer garment. The blood stained garment was horrifying to look at. It was a reminder of the payment for redemption from bondage and from sin.

Hearing the Trumpet

Jesus was on the cross for six hours during the time of Passover. He was nailed to the cross at thc third hour (the Jewish first hour is 6:00 A.M., therefore, the third hour would be 9:00 A.M.). He died on the cross at the ninth hour, or, 3:00 P.M. (Matthew 27:45; Mark 15:34; Luke 23:44).

Jesus, if he was positioned in the right direction, could possibly have seen part of the Temple. The Temple, was a massive, majestic, beautiful edifice on the south side of the Mount Moriah. This was the same location Abraham bound Isaac (Genesis 22). The place of persecution was outside of the city walls on the north side of Mount Moriah. This was the same place Stephen was stoned to death (Acts 7).

Jesus would have heard the priest blow the shofar (trumpet). He would have known it was 3:00 P.M., the time for the sacrifice of the Passover Lamb. The time, when the lamb's throat was slit and the blood was spilled and offered upon the Altar to the Lord.

When Jesus heard the trumpet sound, he said, "It is finished." Jesus chose the moment, the hour, the very minute to die. No man took His life. He laid it down himself. Three days later He took it back and rose again from the dead.

The Passion

After the resurrection Peter stated to a crowd of people in the Temple that "God before had [foretold] by the mouth of all his prophets, that Christ should suffer, he hath so fulfilled" (Acts 3:18). The Prophets told of the Messiah, that He should suffer and rise again.

It was the passion of God to become man, suffer, die and rise again. Ignatius of Antioch, a disciple of the apostles, was being led to Rome in chains. His crime? He was a believer in Jesus as the Messiah. As he was being carted off he wrote letters to the first Christian churches. He spoke of many things regarding his faith and what he had learned from the Apostles.

He was to be thrown to the beasts. He was to be martyred. He wrote, "Do not have Jesus Christ on your lips, and the world in your heart…I am yearning for death with all the passion of a lover" (The Epistle to Romans, 7; Early Christian Writings, Penguin Books, 1968, Maxwell Staniforth, p. 106).

You see, his desire was to please God and to win the crown. He also stated, "All the ends of the earth, all the kingdoms of the world would be of no profit to me; so far as I am concerned, to die in Jesus Christ is better than to be monarch of earth's widest bounds. He who died for us is all that I see; He who rose again for us is my whole desire… Leave me to imitate the Passion of my God" (The Epistle to Romans, 6; Early Christian Writings, Penguin Books, 1968, Maxwell Staniforth, p. 105). Ignatius was quoting Luke writing from Acts 1:3 referencing the resurrected Christ, "To who also he shewed himself alive after his passion by many infallible proofs…" Thus we find the historicity of the term, "the Passion".

When we think of the cross, we must remember the great cost of redemption. Though we may not fully understand as to why this was God's plan, or, God's "passion", nevertheless, His plan is perfect.

Because of the death, burial and resurrection of our Lord Messiah Jesus anyone who believes and turns to Jesus for salvation will receive:

1. *Eternal life* (John 3:16; 10:28)
2. *Forgiveness of sin* (Luke 7:47,48; Ephesians 1:7)
3. *Hope* (Titus 2:13; Revelation 22:20)
4. *Peace* (John 14:27; Philippians 4:7)
5. *Friendship with God* (John 15:15
6. *Name recorded in Heaven* (Luke 10:20)
7. *The Hope of resurrection* (1 Corinthians 15)

The list goes on and on. You get the idea.

Jesus became our Passover Lamb and at the right moment, by His own choosing, Christ died. Three days later He rose again.

What a blessed story! What a marvelous hope Christians have. May our hearts be stirred to live for Him who died for us and rose again. God's love is profound and He wants to have a personal relationship with you, through His Son, the Lord Jesus.

Jesus was forsaken, so we, who believe, may never be forsaken. Jesus bore our sin and died, shedding His blood, so that we, who believe, may be forgiven. Jesus rose again, so that we, who believe, may have eternal life. *This is God's Passion!*

"For God so loved the world, that he gave his only begotten Son, that whosoever believeth in him should not perish, but have everlasting life." John 3:16